The Talent Quest

Story by Jenny Giles
Illustrations by Rachel Tonkin

"We all enjoyed listening to your song, girls," said Miss Bell, when Zoë, Kylie and Megan had finished singing to the class. "I think you should enter the Children's Talent Quest. It's going to be held at the Downtown Shopping Centre during the school holidays."

"Oh, no!" said Megan. "I'd be too nervous to sing at the shopping centre!"

"No, you wouldn't, Megan," said Kylie. "We'd be there to help you."

"Yes," said Zoë, "and we'll practise every day so that we'll be good enough."

"A talent quest!" said Luke. "You know, I can sing that song."

"So can I," said Andrew. "My dad plays it on his guitar."

"This is our song!" said Kylie. "We don't need you two."

Megan looked at Kylie. "But it might sound better with some more voices," she suggested.

"And they're both good singers," added Zoë.

"Well," said Kylie slowly. "I suppose we could see how it sounds."

They all sang the song through together, and Miss Bell said, "That sounded even better than before!"

"Hey!" grinned Luke. "We made a big difference to the group, didn't we, Andrew?"

"We all sang well together," said Andrew quickly, before the girls could argue, "so let's enter for the talent quest."

"All right," said Kylie. "Let's do it!"

The next day at school, Andrew said, "Mum says that you can come and practise at our place, and Dad says that he'll play his guitar for us to sing to."

"But wait a minute!" said Kylie. "Your dad won't be able to play for us at the talent quest. It's only for children."

"I know," replied Andrew, "but we're allowed to have a backing tape, and Dad says he'll play our song through and record it."

"And our song would sound much better with some music," said Megan.

So the following Saturday, they all went to Andrew's house to practise. They sang together while Andrew's dad played his guitar.

Andrew's mum listened to them. Then she said, "I could teach the girls how to sing a different melody for the last chorus, if you like. Then you could harmonise at the end of your song."

"That's a good idea," said Andrew's dad. "What do you all think?"

The children looked at each other and nodded. The girls went into another room with Andrew's mum to learn the new melody, while the boys kept practising.

Soon they were ready to try the song together. When they got to the last chorus, Andrew's mum gave the girls a signal, and they started to sing their melody.

But that made the boys go out of tune. They stopped singing, and the girls forgot their melody. Everyone started to laugh.

"That was terrible!" groaned Luke.

"We'll **never** win if we sound like that!" said Megan.

"More practice needed!" said Andrew's dad.

So they tried again, and again, and again... and then, suddenly, they got it right.

"Hooray!" they all yelled. "We've done it!"

"We can harmonise at last!" cried Kylie.

"And it sounded wonderful!" said Andrew's mum.

On the day of the talent quest, the shopping centre was packed with people. Most of them were gathered around a stage that had been set up near the escalators.

"Oh, no!" cried Megan. "Just look at the crowd! I can't sing in front of all these people!"

"Of course you can, Megan," said Kylie. "We'll be up there with you."

The children were shown where to go, and told that they were last on the program. They sat down and waited for the first item to begin.

A small girl played the violin, and after that an older girl sang.

Then a boy began to play the piano, and the crowd fell silent as the beautiful music echoed through the centre.

"He was **very** good!" whispered Andrew, as the boy took a bow and the audience applauded loudly. The children listened to some more performers, and then, at last, the announcer beckoned to them.

Kylie and Zoë looked at Megan. Then they took her by the hand, and the five children went up onto the stage.

They could see hundreds of people. There were faces gazing down at them from upstairs, and faces staring up at them from below the stage.

"Help!" said Zoë. "**I'm** nervous now!"

"Well, I'm terrified," said Megan, "and my voice is going all shaky!"

"I think I've forgotten the song!" said Luke.

"Hey!" said Kylie. "Look down there in the front row." They all looked down at the crowd.

And there, in the front seats, they could see Miss Bell and some of the boys and girls from their class. They were smiling and waving at them.

The children looked at each other. "Come on!" said Kylie. "We can do it!"

They clipped on their microphones, and began to sing.

The audience listened in silence as the clear notes of the song rang out.

The children came to the last chorus and began to sing the two melodies together. They harmonised perfectly, and when they reached the end of the song, the audience clapped and cheered and whistled loudly.

The crowd was still applauding when the announcer came up onto the stage. He smiled at everyone and held up his hands for silence. "The judges have had a very difficult decision to make," he said, "and I would like Josef, who played the piano so well, to come up onto the stage."

"And now, here they are… the joint winners of this year's Children's Talent Quest… Josef, and the group who just sang to us… Zoë… Megan… Kylie… Luke… and Andrew!"